The Power of Being Cheerful

by Orison Swett Marden

What Vanderbilt Paid for Twelve Laughs

*

William K. Vanderbilt, when he last visited Constantinople, one day invited Coquelin the elder, so celebrated for his powers as a mimic, who happened to be in the city at the time, to give a private recital on board his yacht, lying in the Bosphorus. Coquelin spoke three of his monologues. A few days afterwards Coquelin received the following memorandum from the millionaire:—

"You have brought tears to our eyes and laughter to our hearts. Since all philosophers are agreed that laughing is preferable to weeping, your account with me stands thus:—

"For tears, six times . . . $600
"For laughter, twelve times . . $2,400
_____

$3,000

"Kindly acknowledge receipt of enclosed check."

"I find nonsense singularly refreshing," said Talleyrand. There is good philosophy in the saying, "Laugh and grow fat." If everybody knew the power of laughter as a health tonic and life prolonger the tinge of sadness which now clouds the American face would largely disappear, and many physicians would find their occupation gone.

The power of laughter was given us to serve a wise purpose in our economy. It is Nature's device for exercising the internal organs and giving us pleasure at the same time.

Laughter begins in the lungs and diaphragm, setting the liver, stomach, and other internal organs into a quick, jelly-like vibration, which gives a pleasant sensation and exercise, almost equal to that of horseback riding. During digestion, the movements of the stomach are similar to churning. Every time you take a full breath, or when you cachinnate well, the diaphragm descends and gives the stomach an extra squeeze and shakes it. Frequent laughing sets the stomach to dancing, hurrying up the digestive process. The heart beats faster, and sends the blood bounding through the body. "There is not," says Dr. Green, "one remotest corner or little inlet of the minute blood-vessels of the human body that does not feel some wavelet from the convulsions occasioned by a good hearty laugh." In medical terms, it stimulates the vasomotor centers, and the spasmodic contraction of the blood-vessels causes the blood to flow quickly. Laughter accelerates the respiration, and gives warmth and glow to the whole system. It brightens the eye, increases the perspiration, expands the chest, forces the poisoned air from the least-used lung cells, and tends to restore that exquisite poise or balance which we call health, which results from the harmonious action of all the functions of the body. This delicate poise, which may be destroyed by a sleepless night, a piece of bad news, by grief or anxiety, is often wholly restored by a good hearty laugh.

There is, therefore, sound sense in the caption,—"Cheerfulness as a Life Power,"—relating as it does to the physical life, as well as the mental and moral; and what we may call

THE LAUGH CURE

is based upon principles recognized as sound by the medical profession—so literally true is the Hebrew proverb that "a merry heart doeth good like a medicine."

"Mirth is God's medicine," said Dr. Oliver Wendell Holmes; "everybody ought to bathe in it. Grim care, moroseness, anxiety,—all the rust of life,—ought to be scoured off by the oil of mirth." Elsewhere he says: "If you are making choice of a physician be sure you get one with a cheerful and serene countenance."

Is not a jolly physician of greater service than his pills? Dr. Marshall Hall frequently prescribed "cheerfulness" for his patients, saying that it is better than anything to be obtained at the apothecary's.

In Western New York, Dr. Burdick was known as the "Laughing Doctor." He always presented the happiest kind of a face; and his good humor was contagious. He dealt sparingly in drugs, yet was very successful.

The London "Lancet," the most eminent medical journal in the world, gives the following scientific testimony to the value of jovialty:—

"This power of 'good spirits' is a matter of high moment to the sick and weakly. To the former, it may mean the ability to survive; to the latter, the possibility of outliving, or living in spite of, a disease. It is, therefore, of the greatest importance to cultivate the highest and most buoyant frame of mind which the conditions will admit. The same energy which takes the form of mental activity is vital to the work of the organism. Mental influences affect the system; and a joyous spirit not only relieves pain, but increases the momentum of life in the body."

Dr. Ray, superintendent of Butler Hospital for the Insane, says in one of his reports, "A hearty laugh is more desirable for mental health than any exercise of the reasoning faculties."

Grief, anxiety, and fear are great enemies of human life. A depressed, sour, melancholy soul, a life which has ceased to believe in its own sacredness, its own power, its own mission, a life which sinks into querulous egotism or vegetating aimlessness, has become crippled and useless. We should fight against every influence which tends to depress the mind, as we would against a temptation to crime. It is undoubtedly true that, as a rule, the mind has power to lengthen the period of youthful and mature strength and beauty, preserving and renewing physical life by a stalwart mental health.

I read the other day of a man in a neighboring city who was given up to die; his relatives were sent for, and they watched at his bedside. But an old acquaintance, who called to see him, assured him smilingly that he was all right and would soon be well. He talked in such a strain that the sick man was forced to laugh; and the effort so roused his system that he rallied, and he was soon well again.

Was it not Shakespere who said that a light heart lives long?

The San Francisco "Argonaut" says that a woman in Milpites, a victim of almost crushing sorrow, despondency, indigestion, insomnia, and kindred ills, determined to throw off the gloom which was making life so heavy a burden to her, and established a rule that she would laugh at least three times a day, whether occasion was presented or not; so she trained herself to laugh heartily at the least provocation, and would retire to her room and make merry by herself. She was soon in excellent health and buoyant spirits; her home became a sunny, cheerful abode.

It was said, by one who knew this woman well, and who wrote an account of the case for a popular magazine, that at first her husband and children were amused at her, and while they respected her determination because of the griefs she bore, they did not enter into the spirit of the plan. "But after awhile," said this woman to me, with a smile, only yesterday, "the funny part of the idea struck my husband, and he began to laugh every time we spoke of it. And when he came home, he would ask me if I had had my 'regular laughs;' and he would laugh when he asked the question, and again when I answered it. My children, then very young, thought 'mamma's notion very queer,' but they laughed at it just the same. Gradually, my children told other children, and they told their parents. My husband spoke of it to our friends, and I rarely met one of them but he or she would laugh and ask me, 'How many of your laughs have you had to-day?' Naturally, they laughed when they asked, and of course that set me laughing. When I formed this apparently strange habit I was weighed down with sorrow, and my rule simply lifted me out of it. I had suffered the most acute indigestion; for years I have not known what it is. Headaches were a daily dread; for over six years I have not had a single pain in the head. My home seems different to me, and I feel a thousand times more interest in its work. My husband is a changed man. My children are called 'the girls who are always laughing,' and, altogether, my rule has proved an inspiration which has worked wonders."

The queen of fashion, however, says that we must never laugh out loud; but since the same tyrannical mistress kills people by corsets, indulges in cosmetics, and is out all night at dancing parties, and in China pinches up the women's feet, I place much less confidence in her views upon the laugh cure for human woes. Yet in all civilized countries it is a fundamental principle of refined manners not to be ill-timed and unreasonably noisy and boisterous in mirth. One who is wise will never violate the proprieties of well-bred people.

"Yet," says a wholesome writer upon health, "we should do something more than to simply cultivate a cheerful, hopeful spirit,—we should cultivate a spirit of mirthfulness that is not only easily pleased and smiling, but that indulges in hearty, hilarious laughter; and if this faculty is not well marked in our organization we should cultivate it, being well assured that hearty, body-shaking laughter will do us good."

Ordinary good looks depend on one's sense of humor,—"a merry heart maketh a cheerful countenance." Joyfulness keeps the heart and face young. A good laugh makes us better friends with ourselves and everybody around us, and puts us into closer touch with what is best and brightest in our lot in life.

Physiology tells the story. The great sympathetic nerves are closely allied; and when one set carries bad news to the head, the nerves reaching the stomach are affected, indigestion comes on, and one's countenance becomes doleful. Laugh when you can; it is

A CHEAP MEDICINE.

Merriment is a philosophy not well understood. The eminent surgeon Chavasse says that we ought to begin with the babies and train children to habits of mirth:—

"Encourage your child to be merry and laugh aloud; a good hearty laugh expands the chest and makes the blood bound merrily along. Commend me to a good laugh,—not to a little snickering laugh, but to one that will sound right through the house. It will not only do your child good, but will be a benefit to all who hear, and be an important means of driving the blues away from a dwelling. Merriment is very catching, and spreads in a remarkable manner, few being able to resist its contagion. A hearty laugh is delightful harmony; indeed, it is the best of all music." "Children without hilarity," says an eminent author, "will never amount to much. Trees without blossoms will never bear fruit."

Hufeland, physician to the King of Prussia, commends the ancient custom of jesters at the king's table, whose quips and cranks would keep the company in a roar.

Did not Lycurgus set up the god of laughter in the Spartan eating-halls? There is no table sauce like laughter at meals. It is the great enemy of dyspepsia.

How wise are the words of the acute Chamfort, that the most completely lost of all days is the one in which we have not laughed!

"A crown, for making the king laugh," was one of the items of expense which the historian Hume found in a manuscript of King Edward II.

"It is a good thing to laugh, at any rate," said Dryden, the poet, "and if a straw can tickle a man, it is an instrument of happiness."

"I live," said Laurence Sterne, one of the greatest of English humorists, "in a constant endeavor to fence against the infirmities of ill health and other evils by mirth; I am persuaded that, every time a man smiles,—but much more so when he laughs,—it adds something to his fragment of life."

"Give me an honest laugher," said Sir Walter Scott, and he was himself one of the happiest men in the world, with a kind word and pleasant smile for every one, and everybody loved him.

"How much lies in laughter!" exclaimed the critic Carlyle. "It is the cipher-key wherewith we decipher the whole man. Some men wear an everlasting barren simper; in the smile of others lies the cold glitter, as of ice; the fewest are able to laugh what can be called laughing, but only sniff and titter and snicker from the throat outward, or at least produce some whiffing, husky cachinnation, as if they were laughing through wool. Of none such comes good."

"The power to laugh, to cease work and begin to frolic and make merry in forgetfulness of all the conflict of life," says Campbell Morgan, "is a divine bestowment upon man."

Happy, then, is the man, who may well laugh to himself over his good luck, who can answer the old question, "How old are you?" by Sambo's reply:—

"If you reckon by the years, sah, I'se twenty-five; but if you goes by the fun I's 'ad, I guess I's a hundred."

WHY DON'T YOU LAUGH?

Fromthe"Independent"

"Why don't you laugh, young man, when troubles come,
Instead of sitting 'round so sour and glum?
You cannot have all play,
And sunshine every day;
When troubles come, I say, why don't you laugh?

"Why don't you laugh? 'T will ever help to soothe
The aches and pains. No road in life is smooth;
There's many an unseen bump,
And many a hidden stump
O'er which you'll have to jump. Why don't you laugh?

"Why don't you laugh? Don't let your spirits wilt;
Don't sit and cry because the milk you've spilt;
If you would mend it now,
Pray let me tell you how:
Just milk another cow! Why don't you laugh?

"Why don't you laugh, and make us all laugh, too,
And keep us mortals all from getting blue?
A laugh will always win;

If you can't laugh, just grin,—
Come on, let's all join in! Why don't you laugh?"

II - The Cure for Americanitis

*

Prince Wolkonsky, during a visit to this country, declared that "Business is the alpha and omega of American life. There is no pleasure, no joy, no satisfaction. There is no standard except that of profit. There is no other country where they speak of a man as worth so many dollars. In other countries they live to enjoy life; here they exist for business." A Boston merchant corroborated this statement by saying he was anxious all day about making money, and worried all night for fear he should lose what he had made.

"In the United States," a distinguished traveler once said, "there is everywhere comfort, but no joy. The ambition of getting more and fretting over what is lost absorb life."

"Every man we meet looks as if he'd gone out to borrow trouble, with plenty of it on hand," said a French lady, upon arriving in New York.

"The Americans are the best-fed, the best-clad, and the best-housed people in the world," says another witness, "but they are the most anxious; they hug possible calamity to their breasts."

"I question if care and doubt ever wrote their names so legibly on the faces of any other population," says Emerson; "old age begins in the nursery."

How quickly we Americans exhaust life! With what panting haste we pursue everything! Every man you meet seems to be late for an appointment. Hurry is stamped in the wrinkles of the national face. We are men of action; we go faster and faster as the years go by, speeding our machinery to the utmost. Bent forms, prematurely gray hair, restlessness and discontent, are characteristic of our age and people. We earn our bread, but cannot digest it; and our over-stimulated nerves soon become irritated, and touchiness follows,—so fatal to a business man, and so annoying in society.

"It is not work that kills men," says Beecher; "it is worry. Work is healthy; you can hardly put more on a man than he can bear. But worry is rust upon the blade. It is not movement that destroys the machinery, but friction."

It is not so much the great sorrows, the great burdens, the great hardships, the great calamities, that cloud over the sunshine of life, as the little petty vexations, insignificant anxieties and fear, the little daily dyings, which render our lives unhappy, and destroy our mental elasticity, without advancing our life-work one inch. "Anxiety never yet bridged any chasm."

"What," asks Dr. George W. Jacoby, in an "Evening Post" interview, "is the ultimate physical effect of worry? Why, the same as that of a fatal bullet-wound or sword-thrust. Worry kills as surely, though not so quickly, as ever gun or dagger did, and more people have died in the last century from sheer worry than have been killed in battle."

Dr. Jacoby is one of the foremost of American brain doctors. "The investigations of the neurologists," he says, "have laid bare no secret of Nature in recent years more startling and interesting than the discovery that worry kills." This is the final, up-to-date word. "Not only is it known," resumes the great neurologist, counting off his words, as it were, on his finger-tips, "that worry kills, but the most minute details of its murderous methods are familiar to modern scientists. It is a common belief of those who have made a special study of the science of brain diseases that hundreds of deaths attributed to other causes each year are due simply to worry. In plain, untechnical language, worry works its irreparable injury through certain cells of the brain life. The insidious inroads upon the system can be best likened to the constant falling of drops of water in one spot. In the brain it is the insistent, never-lost idea, the single, constant thought, centered upon one subject, which in the course of time destroys the brain cells. The healthy brain can cope with occasional worry; it is the iteration and reiteration of disquieting thoughts which the cells of the brain cannot successfully combat.

"The mechanical effect of worry is much the same as if the skull were laid bare and the brain exposed to the action of a little hammer beating continually upon it day after day, until the membranes are disintegrated and the normal functions disabled. The maddening thought that will not be downed, the haunting, ever-present idea that is not or cannot be banished by a supreme effort of the will, is the theoretical hammer which diminishes the vitality of the sensitive nerve organisms, the minuteness of which makes them visible to the eye only under a powerful microscope. The 'worry,' the thought, the single idea grows upon one as time goes on, until the worry victim cannot throw it off. Through this, one set or area of cells is affected. The cells are intimately connected, joined together by little fibres, and they in turn are in close relationship with the cells of the other parts of the brain.

"Worry is itself a species of monomania. No mental attitude is more disastrous to personal achievement, personal happiness, and personal usefulness in the world, than worry and its twin brother, despondency. The remedy for the evil lies in training the will to cast off cares and seek a change of occupation, when the first warning is sounded by Nature in intellectual lassitude. Relaxation is the certain foe of worry, and 'don't fret' one of the healthiest of maxims."

In a life of constant worrying, we are as much behind the times as if we were to go back to use the first steam engines that wasted ninety per cent. of the energy of the coal, instead of having an electric dynamo that utilizes ninety per cent. of the power. Some people waste a large percentage of their energy in fretting and stewing, in useless anxiety, in scolding, in complaining about the weather and the perversity of inanimate things. Others convert nearly all of their energy into power and moral sunshine. He who has learned the true art of living will not waste his energies in friction, which accomplishes nothing, but merely grinds out the machinery of life.

It must be relegated to the debating societies to determine which is the worse—A Nervous Man or

A WORRYING WOMAN.

"I'm awfully worried this morning," said one woman. "What is it?" "Why, I thought of something to worry about last night, and now I can't remember it."

A famous actress once said: "Worry is the foe of all beauty." She might have added: "It is the foe to all health."

"It seems so heartless in me, if I do not worry about my children," said one mother.

Women nurse their troubles, as they do their babies. "Troubles grow larger," said Lady Holland, "by nursing."

The White Knight who carried about a mousetrap, lest he be troubled with mice upon his journeys, was not unlike those who anticipate their burdens.

"He grieves," says Seneca, "more than is necessary, who grieves before it is necessary."

"My children," said a dying man, "during my long life I have had a great many troubles, most of which never happened." A prominent business man in Philadelphia said that his father worried for twenty-five years over an anticipated misfortune which never arrived.

We try to grasp too much of life at once; since we think of it as a whole, instead of living one day at a time. Life is a mosaic, and each tiny piece must be cut and set with skill, first one piece, then another.

A clock would be of no use as a time-keeper if it should become discouraged and come to a standstill by calculating its work a year ahead, as the clock did in Jane Taylor's fable. It is not the troubles of to-day, but those of to-morrow and next week and next year, that whiten our heads, wrinkle our faces, and bring us to a standstill.

"There is such a thing," said Uncle Eben, "as too much foresight. People get to figuring what might happen year after next, and let the fire go out and catch their death of cold, right where they are."

Nervous prostration is seldom the result of present trouble or work, but of work and trouble anticipated. Mental exhaustion comes to those who look ahead, and climb mountains before reaching them. Resolutely build a wall about to-day, and live within the inclosure. The past may have been hard, sad, or wrong,—but it is over.

Why not take a turn about? Instead of worrying over unforeseen misfortune, set out with all your soul to rejoice in the unforeseen blessings of all your coming days. "I find the gayest castles in the air that were ever piled," says Emerson, "far better for comfort and for use than the dungeons in the air that are daily dug and caverned out by grumbling, discontented people."

What is this world but as you take it? Thackeray calls the world a looking-glass that gives back the reflection of one's own face. "Frown at it, and it will look sourly upon you; laugh at it, and it is a jolly companion."

"There is no use in talking," said a woman. "Every time I move, I vow I'll never move again. Such neighbors as I get in with! Seems as though they grow worse and worse." "Indeed?" replied her caller; "perhaps you take the worst neighbor with you when you move."

"In the sudden thunder-storm of Independence Day," says a news correspondent, "we were struck by the contrast between two women, each of whom had had some trying experience with the weather. One came through the rain and hail to take refuge at the railway station, under the swaying and uncertain shelter of an escorting man's umbrella. Her skirts were soaked to the knees, her pink ribbons were limp, the purple of the flowers on her hat ran in streaks down the white silk. And yet, though she was a poor girl and her holiday finery must have been relatively costly, she made the best of it with a smile and cheerful words. The other was well sheltered; but she took the disappointment of her hopes and the possibility of a little spattering from a leaky window with frowns and fault-finding."

"Cries little Miss Fret,
In a very great pet:
'I hate this warm weather; it's horrid to tan!
It scorches my nose,
And it blisters my toes,
And wherever I go I must carry a fan.'

"Chirps little Miss Laugh:
'Why, I couldn't tell half
The fun I am having this bright summer day!
I sing through the hours,
I cull pretty flowers,
And ride like a queen on the sweet-smelling hay.'"

Happily a new era has of late opened for our worried housekeepers, who spend their time in "the half-frantic dusting of corners, spasmodic sweeping, impatient snatching or pushing aside obstacles in the room, hurrying and skurrying upstairs and down cellar." "It is not," says Prentice Mulford, "the work that exhausts them,—it is the mental condition they are in that makes so many old and haggard at forty." All that is needful now to ease up their burdens is to go to

OUR HAWAIIAN PARADISE.

A newspaper correspondent, Annie Laurie, has told us all about the new kind of American girls just added to our country:—

"They are as straight as an arrow, and walk as queens walk in fairy stories; they have great braids of sleek, black hair, soft brown eyes, and gleaming white teeth; they can swim and ride and sing; and they are brown with a skin that shines like bronze ... There isn't a worried woman in Hawaii. The women there can't worry. They don't know how. They eat and sing and laugh, and see the sun and the moon set, and possess their souls in smiling peace.

"If a Hawaii woman has a good dinner, she laughs and invites her friends to eat it with her; if she hasn't a good dinner, she laughs and goes to sleep,—and forgets to be hungry. She doesn't have to worry about what the people in the downstairs flat will think if they don't see the butcher's boy arrive on time. If she can earn the money, she buys a nice, new, glorified Mother Hubbard; and, if she can't get it, she throws the old one into the surf and washes it out, puts a new wreath of fresh flowers in her hair, and starts out to enjoy the morning and the breezes thereof.

"They are not earnest workers; they haven't the slightest idea that they were put upon earth to reform the universe,—they're just happy. They run across great stretches of clear, white sand, washed with resplendent purple waves, and, when the little brown babies roll in the surf, their brown mothers run after them, laughing and splashing like a lot of children. Or, perhaps we see them in gay cavalcades mounted upon garlanded ponies, adorned by white jasmine wreaths with roses and pinks. And here in this paradise of laughter and light hearts and gentle music, there's absolutely nothing to do but to care for the children and old people and to swim or ride. You couldn't start a 'reform circle' to save your life; there isn't a jail in the place, nor a tenement quarter, and there are no outdoor poor. There isn't a woman's club in Honolulu,—not a club. There was a culture circle once for a few days; a Boston woman who went there for her health organized it, but it interfered with afternoon nap-time, so nobody came."

When, hereafter, we talk about worrying women, we must take into account our Hawaiian sisters, if we will average up the amount of worry *per capita*, in our nation.

A WEATHER BREEDER.

It is probably quite within bounds to say that one out of three of our American farming population, women and men, never enjoy a beautiful day without first reminding you that "It is one of those infernal weather breeders."

Habitual fretters see more trouble than others. They are never so well as their neighbors. The weather never suits them. The climate is trying. The winds are too high or too low; it is too hot or too cold, too damp or too dry. The roads are either muddy or dusty.

"I met Mr. N. one wet morning," says Dr. John Todd; "and, bound as I was to make the best of it, I ventured:

"'Good morning. This rain will be fine for your grass crop.'

'Yes, perhaps,' he replied, 'but it is very bad for corn; I don't think we'll have half a crop.'

"A few days later, I met him again. 'This is a fine sun for corn, Mr. N.'

"'Yes,' said he, 'but it's awful for rye; rye wants cold weather.'

"One cool morning soon after, I said: 'This is a capital day for rye.'

"'Yes,' he said, 'but it is the worst kind of weather for corn and grass; they want heat to bring them forward.'"

There are a vast number of fidgety, nervous, and eccentric people who live only to expect new disappointments or to recount their old ones.

"Impatient people," said Spurgeon, "water their miseries, and hoe up their comforts."

"Let's see," said a neighbor to a farmer, whose wagon was loaded down with potatoes, "weren't we talking together last August?" "I believe so." "At that time, you said corn was all burnt up." "Yes." "And potatoes were baking in the ground." "Yes." "And that your district could not possibly expect more than half a crop." "I remember." "Well, here you are with your wagon loaded down. Things didn't turn out so badly, after all,—eh?" "Well, no-o," said the farmer, as he raked his fingers through his hair, "but I tell you my geese suffered awfully for want of a mud-hole to paddle in."

What is a pessimist but "a man who looks on the sun only as a thing that casts a shadow"?

In Pepys's "Diary" we learn the difference between "eyes shut and ears open," and "ears shut and eyes open." In going from John o' Groat's House to Land's End, a blind man would hear that the country was going to destruction, but a deaf man with eyes open could see great prosperity.

"I dare no more fret than curse or swear," said John Wesley.

"A discontented mortal is no more a man than discord is music."

"Why should a man whose blood is warm within
Sit like his grandsire cut in alabaster?

Sleep when he wakes? and creep into the jaundice
By being peevish?"

Who are the "lemon squeezers of society"? They are people who predict evil, extinguish hope, and see only the worst side,—"people whose very look curdles the milk and sets your teeth on edge." They are often worthy people who think that pleasure is wrong; people, said an old divine, who lead us heavenward and stick pins into us all the way. They say depressing things and do disheartening things; they chill prayer-meetings, discourage charitable institutions, injure commerce, and kill churches; they are blowing out lights when they ought to be kindling them.

A man without mirth is like a wagon without springs, in which one jolts over every pebble; with mirth, he is like a chariot with springs, riding over the roughest roads and scarcely feeling anything but a pleasant rocking motion.

"Difficulties melt away before the man who carries about a cheerful spirit and persistently refuses to be discouraged, while they accumulate before the one who is always groaning over his hard luck and scanning the horizon for clouds not yet in sight."

"To one man," says Schopenhauer, "the world is barren, dull, and superficial; to another, rich, interesting, and full of meaning." If one loves beauty and looks for it, he will see it wherever he goes. If there is music in his soul, he will hear it everywhere; every object in nature will sing to him. Two men who live in the same house and do the same work may not live in the same world. Although they are under the same roof, one may see only deformity and ugliness; to him the world is out of joint, everything is cross-grained and out of sorts: the other is surrounded with beauty and harmony; everybody is kind to him; nobody wishes him harm. These men see the same objects, but they do not look through the same glasses; one looks through a smoked glass which drapes the whole world in mourning, the other looks through rose-colored lenses which tint everything with loveliness and touch it with beauty.

Take two persons just home from a vacation. "One has positively seen nothing, and has always been robbed; the landlady was a harpy, the bedroom was unhealthy, and the mutton was tough. The other has always found the coziest nooks, the cheapest houses, the best landladies, the finest views, and the best dinners."

"WHAT IS AN OPTIMIST?"

This is the question a farmer's boy asked of his father.

"Well, John," replied his father, "you know I can't give ye the dictionary meanin' of that word any more 'n I can of a great many others. But I've got a kind of an idee what it means. Probably you don't remember your Uncle Henry; but I guess if there ever was an optimist, he was one. Things was always comin' out right with Henry, and especially anything hard that he had to do; it wa' n't a-goin' to be hard,—'t was jest kind of solid-pleasant.

"Take hoein' corn, now. If anything ever tuckered me out, 'twas hoein' corn in the hot sun. But in the field, 'long about the time I begun to lag back a little, Henry he'd look up an' say:—

"'Good, Jim! When we get these two rows hoed, an' eighteen more, the piece'll be half done.' An' he'd say it in such a kind of a cheerful way that I couldn't 'a' ben any more tickled if the piece had been all done,—an' the rest would go light enough.

"But the worst thing we had to do—hoein corn was a picnic to it—was pickin' stones. There was no end to that on our old farm, if we wanted to raise anything. When we wa'n't hurried and pressed with somethin' else, there was always pickin' stones to do; and there wa'n't a plowin' but what brought up a fresh crop, an' seems as if the pickin' had all to be done over again.

"Well, you'd' a' thought, to hear Henry, that there wa'n't any fun in the world like pickin' stones. He looked at it in a different way from anybody I ever see. Once, when the corn was all hoed, and the grass wa'n't fit to cut yet, an' I'd got all laid out to go fishin', and father he up and set us to pickin' stones up on the west piece, an' I was about ready to cry, Henry he says:—

"'Come on, Jim. I know where there's lots of nuggets.'

"An' what do you s'pose, now? That boy had a kind of a game that that there field was what he called a plasser mining field; and he got me into it, and I could 'a' sworn I was in Californy all day,—I had such a good time.

"'Only,' says Henry, after we'd got through the day's work, 'the way you get rich with these nuggets is to get rid of 'em, instead of to get 'em.'

"That somehow didn't strike my fancy, but we'd had play instead of work, anyway, an' a great lot of stones had been rooted out of that field.

"An', as I said before, I can't give ye any dictionary definition of optimism; but if your Uncle Henry wa'n't an optimist, I don't know what one is."

At life's outset, says one, a cheerful optimistic temperament is worth everything. A cheerful man, who always "feels first-rate," who always looks on the bright side, who is ever ready to snatch victory from defeat, is the successful man.

Everybody avoids the company of those who are always grumbling, who are full of "ifs" and "buts," and "I told you so's." We like the man who always looks toward the sun, whether it shines or not. It is the cheerful, hopeful man we go to for sympathy and assistance; not the carping, gloomy critic,—who always thinks it is going to rain, and that we are going to have a terribly hot summer, or a fearful thunder-storm, or who is forever complaining of hard times and his hard lot. It is the bright, cheerful, hopeful, contented man who makes his way, who is respected and admired.

Gloom and depression not only take much out of life, but detract greatly from the chances of winning success. It is the bright and cheerful spirit that wins the final triumph.

LIVING UP THANKSGIVING AVENUE.

"I see our brother, who has just sat down, lives on Grumbling street," said a keen-witted Yorkshireman. "I lived there myself for some time, and never enjoyed good health. The air was bad, the house bad, the water bad; the birds never came and sang in the street; and I was gloomy and sad enough. But I 'flitted.' I got into Thanksgiving avenue; and ever since then I have had good health, and so have all my family. The air is pure, the house good; the sun shines on it all day; the birds are always singing; and I am happy as I can live. Now, I recommend our brother to 'flit.' There are plenty of houses to let on Thanksgiving avenue; and he will find himself a new man if he will only come; and I shall be right glad to have him for a neighbor."

This world was not intended for a "vale of tears," but as a sweet Vale of Content. Travelers are told by the Icelanders, who live amid the cold and desolation of almost perpetual winter, that "Iceland is the best land the sun shines upon." "In the long Arctic night, the Eskimo is blithe, and carolsome, far from the approach of the white man; while amid the glorious scenery and Eden-like climate of Central America, the native languages have a dozen words for pain and misery and sorrow, for one with any cheerful signification."

When a Persian king was directed by his wise men to wear the shirt of a contented man, the only contented man in the kingdom had no shirt. The most contented man in Boston does not live on Commonwealth avenue or do business on State street: he is poor and blind, and he peddles needles and thread, buttons and sewing-room supplies, about the streets of Boston from house to house. Dr. Minot J. Savage used to pity this man very much, and once in venturing to talk with him about his condition, he was utterly amazed to find that the man was perfectly happy. He said that he had a faithful wife, and a business by which he earned sufficient for his wants; and, if he were to complain of his lot, he should feel mean and contemptible. Surely, if there are any "solid men" in Boston, he is one.

Content is the magic lamp, which, according to the beautiful picture painted for us by Goethe, transforms the rude fisherman's hut into a palace of silver; the logs, the floors, the roof, the furniture, everything being changed and gleaming with new light.

"My crown is in my heart, not on my head;
Not decked with diamonds and Indian stones,
Nor to be seen; my crown is called content;
A crown it is that seldom kings enjoy."

III - Oiling Your Business Machinery

*

Business is king. We often say that cotton is king, or corn is king, but with greater propriety we may say that the king is that great machine which is kept in motion by the Law of Supply and Demand: the destinies of all mankind are ruled by it.

"Were the question asked," says Stearns, "what is at this moment the strongest power in operation for controlling, regulating, and inciting the actions of men, what has most at its disposal the condition and destinies of the world, we must answer at once, it is business, in its various ranks and departments; of which commerce, foreign and domestic, is the most appropriate representation. In all prosperous and advancing communities,—advancing in arts, knowledge, literature, and social refinement,—business is king. Other influences in society may be equally indispensable, and some may think far more dignified, but *Business is King*. The statesman and the scholar, the nobleman and the prince, equally with the manufacturer, the mechanic, and the laborer, pursue their several objects only by leave granted and means furnished by this potentate."

Oil is better than sand for keeping this vast machinery in good running condition. Do not shovel grit or gravel stones upon the bearings. A tiny copper shaving in a wheel box, or a scratch on a journal, may set a railway train on fire. The running of the business world is damaged by whatever creates friction.

Anxiety mars one's work. Nobody can do his best when, fevered by worry. One may rush, and always be in great haste, and may talk about being busy, fuming and sweating as if he were doing ten men's duties; and yet some quiet person alongside, who is moving leisurely and without anxious haste, is probably accomplishing twice as much, and doing it better. Fluster unfits one for good work.

Have you not sometimes seen a business manager whose stiffness would serve as "a good example to a poker?" He acts toward his employees as the father of Frederick the Great did toward his subjects, caning them on the streets, and shouting, "I wish to be loved and not feared." "Growl, Spitfire and Brothers," says Talmage, "wonder why they fail, while Messrs. Merriman and Warmheart succeed."

There is no investment a business man can make that will pay him a greater per cent, than patience and amiability. Good humor will sell the most goods.

John Wanamaker's clerks have been heard to say: "We can work better for a week after a pleasant 'Good morning' from Mr. Wanamaker."

This kindly disposition and cheerful manner, and a desire to create a pleasant feeling and diffuse good cheer among those who work for him, have had a great deal to do with the great merchant's remarkable success. On the other hand, a man who easily finds fault, and is never generous-spirited, who never commends the work of subordinates when he can do so justly, who is unwilling to brighten their hours, fails to secure the best of service. "Why not try love's way?" It will pay better, and be better.

A habit of cheerfulness, enabling one to transmute apparent misfortunes into real blessings, is a fortune to a young man or young woman just crossing the threshold of active life. There is nothing but ill fortune in a habit of grumbling, which "requires no talent, no self-denial, no brains, no character." Grumbling only makes an employee more uncomfortable, and may cause his dismissal. No one would or should wish to make him do grudgingly what so many others would be glad to do in a cheerful spirit.

If you dislike your position, complain to no one, least of all to your employer. Fill the place as it was never filled before. Crowd it to overflowing. Make yourself more competent for it. Show that you are abundantly worthy of better things. Express yourself in this manner as freely as you please, for it is the only way that will count.

No one ever found the world quite as he would like it. You will be sure to have burdens laid upon you that belong to other people, unless you are a shirk yourself; but don't grumble. If the work needs doing and you can do it, never mind about the other one who ought to have done it and didn't; do it yourself. Those workers who fill up the gaps, and smooth away the rough spots, and finish up the jobs that others leave undone,—they are the true peacemakers, and worth a regiment of grumblers.

"Oh, what a sunny, winsome face she has!" said a Christian Endeavorer, in reporting of a clerk whom he saw in a Bay City store. "The customers flocked about her like bees about a honey-bush in full bloom."

SINGING AT YOUR WORK.

"Give us, therefore,"—let us cry with Carlyle,—"oh, give us the man who sings at his work! He will do more in the same time, he will do it better, he will persevere longer. One is scarcely sensible of fatigue whilst he marches to music. The very stars are said to make harmony as they revolve in their spheres. Wondrous is the strength of cheerfulness, altogether past calculation its powers of endurance. Efforts, to be permanently useful, must be uniformly joyous, a spirit all sunshine, graceful from very gladness, beautiful because bright."

"It is a good sign," says another writer, "when girlish voices carol over the steaming dish-pan or the mending-basket, when the broom moves rhythmically, and the duster flourishes in time to some brisk melody. We are sure that the dishes shine more brightly, and that the sweeping and dusting and mending are more satisfactory because of this running accompaniment of song. Father smiles when he hears his girl singing about her work, and mother's tired face brightens at the sound. Brothers and sisters, without realizing it, perhaps, catch the spirit of the cheerful worker."

There are singing milkers in Switzerland; a milkmaid or man gets better wages if gifted with a good voice, for a cow will yield one-fifth more milk when soothed by a pleasing melody.

It was said by Buffon that even sheep fatten better to the sound of music. And when field-hands are singing, as you sometimes hear them in the old country, you may be sure the labor is lightened.

It is Mrs. Howitt who has told us of the musical bells of the farm teams in a rural district in England:—"It was no regular tune, but a delicious melody in that soft, sunshiny air, which was filled at the same time with the song of birds. Angela had heard all kinds of music in London, but this was unlike anything she had heard before, so soft, and sweet, and gladsome. On it came, ringing, ringing as softly as flowing water. The boys and grandfather knew what it meant. Then it came in sight,—the farm team going to the mill with sacks of corn to be ground, each horse with a little string of bells to its harness. On they came, the handsome, well-cared-for creatures, nodding their heads as they stepped along; and at every step the cheerful and cheering melody rang out.

"'Do all horses down here have bells?' asked Angela.

"'By no means,' replied her grandfather. 'They cost something; but if we can make labor easier to a horse by giving him a little music, which he loves, he is less worn by his work, and that is a saving worth thinking of. A horse is a generous, noble-spirited animal, and not without intellect, either; and he is capable of much enjoyment from music.'"

A spirit of song, if not the singing itself, is a constant delight to us. "It is like passing sweet meadows alive with bobolinks."

"Some men," says Beecher, "move through life as a band of music moves down the street, flinging out pleasures on every side, through the air, to every one far and near who can listen; others fill the air with harsh clang and clangor. Many men go through life carrying their tongue, their temper, their whole disposition so that wherever they go, others dread them. Some men fill the air with their presence and sweetness, as orchards in October days fill the air with the perfume of ripe fruit."

GOOD HUMOR.

"Health and good humor," said Massillon, "are to the human body like sunshine to vegetation."

The late Charles A. Dana fairly bubbled over with the enjoyment of his work, and was, up to his last illness, at his office every day. A Cabinet officer once said to him: "Well, Mr. Dana, I don't see how you stand this infernal grind."

"Grind?" said Mr. Dana. "You never were more mistaken. I have nothing but fun."

"Bully" was a favorite word with him; a slang word used to express uncommon pleasure, such as had been afforded by a trip abroad, or by a run to Cuba or Mexico, or by the perusal of something especially pleasing in the "Sun's" columns.

"One of my neighbors is a very ill-tempered man," said Nathan Rothschild. "He tries to vex me, and has built a great place for swine close to my walk. So, when I go out, I hear first, 'Grunt, grunt,' then 'Squeak, squeak.' But this does me no harm. I am always in good humor."

Offended by a pungent article, a gentleman called at the "Tribune" office and inquired for the editor. He was shown into a little seven-by-nine sanctum, where Greeley sat, with his head close down to his paper, scribbling away at a two-forty rate. The angry man began by asking if this was Mr. Greeley. "Yes, sir; what do you want?" said the editor quickly, without once looking up from his paper. The irate visitor then began using his tongue, with no reference to the rules of propriety, good breeding, or reason. Meantime Mr. Greeley continued to write. Page after page was dashed off in the most impetuous style, with no change of features, and without paying the slightest attention to the visitor. Finally, after about twenty minutes of the most impassioned scolding ever poured out in an editor's office, the angry man became disgusted, and abruptly turned to walk out of the room. Then, for the first time, Mr. Greeley quickly looked up, rose from his chair, and, slapping the gentleman familiarly on his shoulder, in a pleasant tone of voice said: "Don't go, friend; sit down, sit down, and free your mind; it will do you good,—you will feel better for it. Besides, it helps me to think what I am to write about. Don't go."

"One good hearty laugh," says Talmage, "is like a bomb-shell exploding in the right place, and spleen and discontent like a gun that kicks over the man shooting it off."

"Every one," says Lubbock, "likes a man who can enjoy a laugh at his own expense,—and justly so, for it shows good humor and good sense. If you laugh at yourself, other people will not laugh at you."

People differ very much in their sense of humor. As some are deaf to certain sounds and blind to certain colors, so there are those who seem deaf and blind to certain pleasures. What makes me laugh until I almost go into convulsions moves them not at all.

Is it not worth while to make an effort to see the funny side of our petty annoyances? How could the two boys but laugh, after they had contended long over the possession of a box found by the wayside, when they agreed to divide its contents, and found nothing in it?

The ability to get on with scolding, irritating people is a great art in doing business. To preserve serenity amid petty trials is a happy gift.

A sunny temper is also conducive to health. A medical authority of highest repute affirms that "excessive labor, exposure to wet and cold, deprivation of sufficient quantities of necessary and wholesome food, habitual bad lodging, sloth, and intemperance are all deadly enemies to human life, but they are none of them so bad as violent and ungoverned passions;" that men and women have frequently lived to an advanced age in spite of these; but that instances are very rare in which people of irascible tempers live to extreme old age.

Poultney Bigelow, in "Harper's Magazine," in relating the story of Jameson's raid upon the Boers of South Africa, says that the triumphant Boers fell on their knees, thanking God for their victory; and that they prayed for their enemies, and treated their prisoners with the utmost kindness. Our foreign missionary books relate similar anecdotes, it being a characteristic feature of their childlike piety for new converts to take literally the words of our Lord,—"Love your enemies."

It is not true that the devil has his tail in everything. A stalwart confidence in God, and faith in the happy outcome of life, will do more to lubricate the creaking machinery of our daily affairs than anything else.

"LE DIABLE EST MORT."

"*Courage, ami, le diable est mort!*" "Courage, friend, the devil is dead!" was Denys's constant countersign, which he would give to everybody. "They don't understand it," he would say, "but it wakes them up. I carry the good news from city to city, to uplift men's hearts." Once he came across a child who had broken a pitcher. "*Courage, amie, le diable est mort!*" said he, which was such cheering news that she ceased crying, and ran home to tell it to her grandma.

Give me the man who, like Emerson, sees longevity in his cause, and who believes there is a remedy for every wrong, a satisfaction for every longing soul; the man who believes the best of everybody, and who sees beauty and grace where others see ugliness and deformity. Give me the man who believes in the ultimate triumph of truth over error, of harmony over discord, of love over hate, of purity over vice, of light over darkness, of life over death. Such men are the true nation-builders.

Jay Cooke, many times a millionaire at the age of fifty-one, at fifty-two practically penniless, went to work again and built another fortune. The last of his three thousand creditors was paid, and the promise of the great financier was fulfilled. To a visitor who once asked him how he regained his fortune, Mr. Cooke replied, "That is simple enough: by never changing the temperament I derived from my father and mother. From my earliest experience in life I have always been of a hopeful temperament, never living in a cloud; I have always had a reasonable philosophy to think that men and times are better than harsh criticism would suppose. I believed that this American world of ours is full of wealth, and that it was only necessary to go to work and find it. That is the secret of my success in life. Always look on the sunny side."

"Everything has gone," said a New York business man in despair, when he reached home. But when he came to himself he found that his wife and his children and the promises of God were left to him. Suffering, it was said by Aristotle, becomes beautiful when any one bears great calamities with cheerfulness, not through insensibility, but through greatness of mind.

When Garrison was locked up in the Boston city jail he said he had two delightful companions,—a good conscience and a cheerful mind.

"To live as always seeing
The invisible Source of things,
Is the blessedest state of being,
For the quietude it brings."

"Away with those fellows who go howling through life," wrote Beccher, "and all the while passing for birds of paradise! He that cannot laugh and be gay should look to himself. He should fast and pray until his face breaks forth into light."

Martin Luther has told us that he was once sorely discouraged and vexed at himself, the world, and the church, and at the small success he then seemed to be having; and he fell into a despondency which affected all his household. His good wife could not charm it away by cheerful speech or acts. At length she hit upon this happy device, which proved effectual. She appeared before him in deep mourning.

"Who is dead?" asked Luther.

"Oh, do you not know, Martin? God in heaven is dead."

"How can you talk such nonsense, Kaethe? How can God die? Why, He is immortal, and will live through all eternity."

"Is that really true?" persisted she, as if she could hardly credit his assertion that God still lived.

"How can you doubt it? So surely as there is a God in heaven," asserted the aroused theologian, "so sure is it that He can never die."

"And yet," said she demurely, in a tone which made him look up at her, "though you do not doubt there is a God, you become hopeless and discouraged as if there were none. It seemed to me you acted as if God were dead."

The spell was broken; Luther heartily laughed at his wife's lesson, and her ingenious way of presenting it. "I observed," he remarked, "what a wise woman my wife was, who mastered my sadness."

Jean Paul Richter's dream of "No God" is one of the most somber things in all literature,—"tempestuous chaos, no healing hand, no Infinite Father. I awoke. My soul wept for joy that it could again worship the Infinite Father.... And when I arose, from all nature I heard flowing sweet, peaceful tones, as from evening bells."

IV - Taking Your Fun Every Day as You Do Your Work

*

Ten things are necessary for happiness in this life, the first being a good digestion, and the other nine,—money; so at least it is said by our modern philosophers. Yet the author of "A Gentle Life" speaks more truly in saying that the Divine creation includes thousands of superfluous joys which are totally unnecessary to the bare support of life.

He alone is the happy man who has learned to extract happiness, not from ideal conditions, but from the actual ones about him. The man who has mastered the secret will not wait for ideal surroundings; he will not wait until next year, next decade, until he gets rich, until he can travel abroad, until he can afford to surround himself with works of the great masters; but he will make the most out of life to-day, where he is.

"Why thus longing, thus forever sighing,
For the far-off, unattained and dim,
While the beautiful, all round thee lying,
Offers up its low, perpetual hymn?

"Happy the man, and happy he alone,
He who can call to-day his own;
He who, secure within himself, can say:
'To-morrow, do thy worst, for I have lived to-day!'"

Paradise is here or nowhere: you must take your joy with you or you will never find it.

It is after business hours, not in them, that men break down. Men must, like Philip Armour, turn the key on business when they leave it, and at once unlock the doors of some wholesome recreation. Dr. Lyman Beecher used to divert himself with a violin. He had a regular system of what he called "unwinding," thus relieving the great strain put upon him.

"A man," says Dr. Johnson, "should spend part of his time with the laughers."

Humor was Lincoln's life-preserver, as it has been of thousands of others. "If it were not for this," he used to say, "I should die." His jests and quaint stories lighted the gloom of dark hours of national peril.

"Next to virtue," said Agnes Strickland, "the fun in this world is what we can least spare."

"When the harness is off," said Judge Haliburton, "a critter likes to kick up his heels."

"I have fun from morning till night," said the editor Charles A. Dana to a friend who was growing prematurely old. "Do you read novels, and play billiards, and walk a great deal?"

Gladstone early formed a habit of looking on the bright side of things, and never lost a moment's sleep by worrying about public business.

There are many out-of-door sports, and the very presence of nature is to many a great joy. How true it is that, if we are cheerful and contented, all nature smiles with us,—the air seems more balmy, the sky more clear, the earth has a brighter green, the trees have a richer foliage, the flowers are more fragrant, the birds sing more sweetly, and the sun, moon, and stars all appear more beautiful. "It is a grand thing to live,—to open the eyes in the morning and look out upon the world, to drink in the pure air and enjoy the sweet sunshine, to feel the pulse bound, and the being thrill with the consciousness of strength and power in every nerve; it is a good thing simply to be alive, and it is a good world we live in, in spite of the abuse we are fond of giving it."

"I love to hear the bee sing amid the blossoms sunny;
To me his drowsy melody is sweeter than his honey:
For, while the shades are shifting
Along the path to noon,
My happy brain goes drifting
To dreamland on his tune.

"I love to hear the wind blow amid the blushing petals,
And when a fragile flower falls, to watch it as it settles;
And view each leaflet falling
Upon the emerald turf,
With idle mind recalling
The bubbles on the surf.

"I love to lie upon the grass, and let my glances wander
Earthward and skyward there; while peacefully I ponder
How much of purest pleasure
Earth holds for his delight
Who takes life's cup to measure
Naught but its blessings bright."

Upon every side of us are to be found what one has happily called—

UNWORKED JOY MINES.

And he who goes "prospecting" to see what he can daily discover is a wise man, training his eye to see beauty in everything and everywhere.

"One ought, every day," says Goethe, "at least to hear a little song, read a good poem, see a fine picture, and, if it were possible, to speak a few reasonable words." And if this be good for one's self, why not try the song, the poem, the picture, and the good words, on some one else?

Shall music and poetry die out of you while you are struggling for that which can never enrich the character, nor add to the soul's worth? Shall a disciplined imagination fill the mind with beautiful pictures? He who has intellectual resources to fall back upon will not lack for daily recreation most wholesome.

It was a remark of Archbishop Whately that we ought not only to cultivate the cornfields of the mind, but the pleasure-grounds also. A well-balanced life is a cheerful life; a happy union of fine qualities and unruffled temper, a clear judgment, and well-proportioned faculties. In a corner of his desk, Lincoln kept a copy of the latest humorous work; and it was frequently his habit, when fatigued, annoyed, or depressed, to take this up, and read a chapter with great relief. Clean, sensible wit, or sheer nonsense,—anything to provoke mirth and make a man jollier,—this, too, is a gift from Heaven.

In the world of books, what is grand and inspiring may easily become a part of every man's life. A fondness for good literature, for good fiction, for travel, for history, and for biography,—what is better than this?

THE QUEEN OF THE WORLD.

This title best fits Victoria, the true queen of the world, but it fits her best because she is the best type of a noble wife, the queen of her husband's heart, and of a queen mother whose children rise up and call her blessed.

"I noticed," said Franklin, "a mechanic, among a number of others, at work on a house a little way from my office, who always appeared to be in a merry humor; he had a kind word and smile for every one he met. Let the day be ever so cold, gloomy, or sunless, a happy smile danced on his cheerful countenance. Meeting him one morning, I asked him to tell me the secret of his constant flow of spirits.

"'It is no secret, doctor,' he replied. 'I have one of the best of wives; and, when I go to work, she always has a kind word of encouragement for me; and, when I go home, she meets me with a smile and a kiss; and then tea is sure to be ready, and she has done so many little things through the day to please me that I cannot find it in my heart to speak an unkind word to anybody.'"

Some of the happiest homes I have ever been in, ideal homes, where intelligence, peace, and harmony dwell, have been homes of poor people. No rich carpets covered the floors; there were no costly paintings on the walls, no piano, no library, no works of art. But there were contented minds, devoted and unselfish lives, each contributing as much as possible to the happiness of all, and endeavoring to compensate by intelligence and kindness for the poverty of their surroundings. "One cheerful, bright, and contented spirit in a household will uplift the tone of all the rest. The keynote of the home is in the hand of the resolutely cheerful member of the family, and he or she will set the pitch for the rest."

"Young men," it is said, "are apt to be overbearing, imperious, brusque in their manner; they need that suavity of manner, and urbanity of demeanor, gracefulness of expression and delicacy of manner, which can only be gained by association with the female character, which possesses the delicate instinct, ready judgment, acute perceptions, wonderful intuition. The blending of the male and female characteristics produces the grandest character in each."

The woman who has what Helen Hunt so aptly called "a genius for affection,"—she, indeed, is queen of the home. "I have often had occasion," said Washington Irving, "to remark the fortitude with which woman sustains the most overwhelming reverses of fortune. Those disasters which break down the spirit of a man, and prostrate him in the dust, seem to call forth all the energies of the softer sex, and give such intrepidity and elevation to their character that at times it approaches sublimity."

If a wife cannot make her home bright and happy, so that it shall be the cleanest, sweetest, cheerfulest place her husband can find refuge in,—a retreat from the toils and troubles of the outer world,—then God help the poor man, for he is virtually homeless. "Home-keeping hearts," said Longfellow, "are happiest." What is a good wife, a good mother? Is she not a gift out of heaven, sacred and delicate, with affections so great that no measuring line short of that of the infinite God can tell their bound; fashioned to refine and soothe and lift and irradiate home and society and the world; of such value that no one can appreciate it, unless his mother lived long enough to let him understand it, or unless, in some great crisis of life, when all else failed him, he had a wife to reenforce him with a faith in God that nothing could disturb?

Nothing can be more delightful than an anecdote of Joseph H. Choate, of New York, our Minister at the Court of St. James. Upon being asked, at a dinner-party, who he would prefer to be if he could not be himself, he hesitated a moment, apparently running over in his mind the great ones on earth, when his eyes rested on Mrs. Choate at the other end of the table, who was watching him with great interest in her face, and suddenly replied, "If I could not be myself, I should like to be Mrs. Choate's second husband."

"Pleasant words are as a honeycomb, sweet to the soul and health to the bones." It is the little disputes, little fault-findings, little insinuations, little reflections, sharp criticisms, fretfulness and impatience, little unkindnesses, slurs, little discourtesies, bad temper, that create most of the discord and unhappiness in the family. How much it would add to the glory of the homes of the world if that might be said of every one which Rogers said of Lord Holland's sunshiny face: "He always comes to breakfast like a man upon whom some sudden good fortune has fallen"!

The value of pleasant words every day, as you go along, is well depicted by Aunt Jerusha in what she said to our genial friend of "Zion's Herald":—

"If folks could have their funerals when they are alive and well and struggling along, what a help it would be"! she sighed, upon returning from a funeral, wondering how poor Mrs. Brown would have felt if she could have heard what the minister said. "Poor soul, she never dreamed they set so much by her!

"Mis' Brown got discouraged. Ye see, Deacon Brown, he'd got a way of blaming everything on to her. I don't suppose the deacon meant it,—'twas just his way,—but it's awful wearing. When things wore out or broke, he acted just as if Mis' Brown did it herself on purpose; and they all caught it, like the measles or the whooping-cough.

"And the minister a-telling how the deacon brought his young wife here when 't wa'n't nothing but a wilderness, and how patiently she bore hardship, and what a good wife she'd been! Now the minister wouldn't have known anything about that if the deacon hadn't told him. Dear! Dear! If he'd only told Mis' Brown herself what he thought, I do believe he might have saved the funeral.

"And when the minister said how the children would miss their mother, seemed as though they couldn't stand it, poor things!

"Well, I guess it is true enough,—Mis' Brown was always doing for some of them. When they was singing about sweet rest in heaven, I couldn't help thinking that that was something Mis' Brown would have to get used to, for she never had none of it here.

"She'd have been awful pleased with the flowers. They was pretty, and no mistake. Ye see, the deacon wa'n't never willing for her to have a flower-bed. He said 't was enough prettier sight to see good cabbages a-growing; but Mis' Brown always kind of hankered after sweet-smelling things, like roses and such.

"What did you say, Levi? 'Most time for supper? Well, land's sake, so it is! I must have got to meditating. I've been a-thinking, Levi, you needn't tell the minister anything about me. If the pancakes and pumpkin pies are good, you just say so as we go along. It ain't best to keep everything laid up for funerals."

It is the grand secret of a happy home to express the affection you really have.

"He is the happiest," it was said by Goethe, "be he king or peasant, who finds peace in his home." There are indeed many serious, too serious-minded fathers and mothers who do not wish to advertise their children to all the neighbors as "the laughing family." If this be so, yet, at the very least, these solemn parents may read the Bible. Where it is said, "provoke not your children to wrath," it means literally, "do not irritate your children;" "do not rub them up the wrong way."

Children ought never to get the impression that they live in a hopeless, cheerless, cold world; but the household cheerfulness should transform their lives like sunlight, making their hearts glad with little things, rejoicing upon small occasion.

"How beautiful would our home-life be if every little child at the bed-time hour could look into the faces of the older ones and say: 'We've had such sweet times to-day.'"

"To love, and to be loved," says Sydney Smith, "is the greatest happiness of existence."

V - Finding What You Do Not Seek

*

Dining one day with Baron James Rothschild, Eugene Delacroix, the famous French artist, confessed that, during some time past, he had vainly sought for a head to serve as a model for that of a beggar in a picture which he was painting; and that, as he gazed at his host's features, the idea suddenly occurred to him that the very head he desired was before him. Rothschild, being a great lover of art, readily consented to sit as the beggar. The next day, at the studio, Delacroix placed a tunic around the baron's shoulders, put a stout staff in his hand, and made him pose as if he were resting on the steps of an ancient Roman temple. In this attitude he was found by one of the artist's favorite pupils, in a brief absence of the master from the room. The youth naturally concluded that the beggar had just been brought in, and with a sympathetic look quietly slipped a piece of money into his hand. Rothschild thanked him simply, pocketed the money, and the student passed out. Rothschild then inquired of the master, and found that the young man had talent, but very slender means. Soon after, the youth received a letter stating that charity bears interest, and that the accumulated interest on the amount he had given to one he supposed to be a beggar was represented by the sum of ten thousand francs, which was awaiting his claim at the Rothschild office.

This illustrates well the art of cheerful amusement even if one has great business cares,—the entertainment of the artist, the personation of a beggar, and an act of beneficence toward a worthy student.

It illustrates, too, what was said by Wilhelm von Humboldt, that "it is worthy of special remark that when we are not too anxious about happiness and unhappiness, but devote ourselves to the strict and unsparing performance of duty, then happiness comes of itself." We carry each day nobly, doing the duty or enjoying the privilege of the moment, without thinking whether or not it will make us happy. This is quite in accord with the saying of George Herbert, "The consciousness of duty performed gives us music at midnight."

Are not buoyant spirits like water sparkling when it runs? "*I have found my greatest happiness in labor*," said Gladstone. "I early formed a habit of industry, and it has been its own reward. The young are apt to think that rest means a cessation from all effort, but I have found the most perfect rest in changing effort. If brain-weary over books and study, go out into the blessed sunlight and the pure air, and give heartfelt exercise to the body. The brain will soon become calm and rested. The efforts of Nature are ceaseless. Even in our sleep the heart throbs on. I try to live close to Nature, and to imitate her in my labors. The compensation is sound sleep, a wholesome digestion, and powers that are kept at their best; and this, I take it, is the chief reward of industry."

"Owing to ingrained habits," said Horace Mann, "work has always been to me what water is to a fish. I have wondered a thousand times to hear people say, 'I don't like this business,' or 'I wish I could exchange it for that;' for with me, when I have had anything to do, I do not remember ever to have demurred, but have always set about it like a fatalist, and it was as sure to be done as the sun was to set."

"*One's personal enjoyment is a very small thing, but one's personal usefulness is a very important thing." Those only are happy who have their minds fixed on some object other than their own happiness.* "The most delicate, the most sensible of all pleasures," says La Bruyere, "consists in promoting the pleasures of others." And Hawthorne has said that the inward pleasure of imparting pleasure is the choicest of all.

"Oh, it is great," said Carlyle, "and there is no other greatness,—to make some nook of God's creation more fruitful, better, more worthy of God,—to make some human heart a little wiser, manlier, happier, more blessed, less accursed!" The gladness of service, of having some honorable share in the world's work, what is better than this?

"The Lord must love the common people," said Lincoln, "for he made so many of them, and so few of the other kind." To extend to all the cup of joy is indeed angelic business, and there is nothing that makes one more beautiful than to be engaged in it.

"The high desire that others may be blest savors of heaven."

The memory of those who spend their days in hanging sweet pictures of faith and trust in the galleries of sunless lives shall never perish from the earth.

DOING GOOD BY STEALTH, AND HAVING IT FOUND OUT BY ACCIDENT.

"This," said Charles Lamb, "is the greatest pleasure I know." "Money never yet made a man happy," said Franklin; "and there is nothing in its nature to produce happiness." To do good with it, makes life a delight to the giver. How happy, then, was the life of Jean Ingelow, since what she received from the sale of a hundred thousand copies of her poems, and fifty thousand of her prose works, she spent largely in charity; one unique charity being a "copyright" dinner three times a week to twelve poor persons just discharged from the neighboring hospitals! Nor was any one made happier by it than the poet.

John Buskin inherited a million dollars. "With this money he set about doing good," says a writer in the "Arena." "Poor young men and women who were struggling to get an education were helped, homes for working men and women were established, and model apartment houses were erected. He also promoted a work for reclaiming waste land outside of London. This land was used for the aid of unfortunate men who wished to rise again from the state in which they had fallen through cruel social conditions and their own weaknesses. It is said that this work suggested to General Booth his colonization farms. Ruskin has also ever been liberal in aiding poor artists, and has done much to encourage artistic taste among the young. On one occasion he purchased ten fine water-color paintings by Holman Hunt for $3,750, to be hung in the public schools of London. By 1877 he had disposed of three-fourths of his inheritance, besides all the income from his books. But the calls of the poor, and his plans looking toward educating and ennobling the lives of working men, giving more sunshine and joy, were such that he determined to dispose of all the remainder of his wealth except a sum sufficient to yield him $1,500 a year on which to live."

Our own Peter Cooper, in his last days, was one of the happiest men in America; his beneficence shone in his countenance.

Let the man who has the blues take a map and census table of the world, and estimate how many millions there are who would gladly exchange lots with him, and let him begin upon some practicable plan to do all the good he can to as many as he can, and he will forget to be despondent; and he need not stop short at praying for them without first giving every dollar he can, without troubling the Lord about that. Let him scatter his flowers as he goes along, since he will never go over the same road again.

No man in England had a better time than did Du Maurier on that cold day when he took the hat of an old soldier on Hampstead road, and sent him away to the soup kitchen in Euston to get warm. The artist chalked on a blackboard such portraits as he commonly made for "Punch," and soon gathered a great quantity of small coins for the grateful soldier; who, however, at once rubbed out Du Maurier's pictures and put on "the faithful dog," and a battle scene, as more artistic.

"Chinese Gordon," after serving faithfully and valiantly in the great Chinese rebellion, and receiving the highest honors of the Chinese Empire, returned to England, caring little for the praise thus heaped on him. He took some position at Gravesend, just below London, where he filled his house with boys from the streets, whom he taught and made men of, and then secured them places on ships,—following them all over the world with letters of advice and encouragement.

HIS HEAD IN A HOLE.

"I was appointed to lecture in a town in Great Britain six miles from the railway," said John B. Gough, "and a man drove me in a fly from the station to the town. I noticed that he sat leaning forward in an awkward manner, with his face close to the glass of the window. Soon he folded a handkerchief and tied it round his neck. I asked him if he was cold. "No, sir." Then he placed the handkerchief round his face. I asked him if he had the toothache. "No, sir," was the reply. Still he sat leaning forward. At last I said, "Will you please tell me why you sit leaning forward that way with a handkerchief round your neck if you are not cold and have no toothache?" He said very quietly, "The window of the carriage is broke, and the wind is cold, and I am trying to keep it from you." I said, in surprise, "You are not putting your face to that broken pane to keep the wind from me, are you?" "Yes, sir, I am." "Why do you do that?" "God bless you, sir! I owe everything I have in the world to you." "But I never saw you before." "No, sir; but I have seen you. I was a ballad-singer once. I used to go round with a half-starved baby in my arms for charity, and a draggled wife at my heels half the time, with her eyes blackened; and I went to hear you in Edinburgh, and *you told me I was a man*; and when I went out of that house I said, 'By the help of God, I'll be a man;' and now I've a happy wife and a comfortable home. God bless you, sir! I would stick my head in any hole under the heavens if it would do you any good."

"Let's find the sunny side of men,
Or be believers in it;
A light there is in every soul
That takes the pains to win it.
Oh! there's a slumbering good in all,
And we perchance may wake it;
Our hands contain the magic wand:
This life is what we make it."

He indeed is getting the most out of life who does most to elevate mankind. How happy were those Little Sisters of the Poor at Tours, who took scissors to divide their last remnant of bedclothing with an old woman who came to them at night, craving hospitality! And how happy was that American school-teacher who gave up the best room in the house, which she had engaged long before the season opened, at a mountain sanitarium, during the late war, taking instead of it the poorest room in the house, that she might give good quarters to a soldier just out of his camp hospital!

"Teach self-denial," said Walter Scott, "and make its practice pleasurable, and you create for the world a destiny more sublime than ever issued from the brain of the wildest dreamer."

Yet how many there are, ready to make some great sacrifice, who neglect those little acts of kindness which make so many lives brighter and happier.

"I say, Jim, it's the first time I ever had anybody ask my parding, and it kind o' took me off my feet." A young lady had knocked him down in hastily turning a corner. She stopped and said to the ragged crossing-boy: "I beg your pardon, my little fellow; I am very sorry I ran against you." He took off the piece of a cap he had on his skull, made a low bow, and said with a broad smile: "You have my parding, Miss, and welcome; and the next time you run agin me, you can knock me clean down and I won't say a word."

One of the greatest mistakes of life is to save our smiles and pleasant words and sympathy for those of "our set," or for those not now with us, and for other times than the present.

"If a word or two will render a man happy," said a Frenchman, "he must be a wretch indeed who will not give it. It is like lighting another man's candle with your own, which loses none of its brilliancy by what the other gains."

Sydney Smith recommends us to make at least one person happy every day: "Take ten years, and you will make thirty-six hundred and fifty persons happy; or brighten a small town by your contribution to the fund of general joy." One who is cheerful is preeminently useful.

Dr. Baffles once said: "I have made it a rule never to be with a person ten minutes without trying to make him happier." It was a remark of Dr. Dwight, that "one who makes a little child happier for half an hour is a fellow-worker with God."

A little boy said to his mother: "I couldn't make little sister happy, nohow I could fix it. But I made myself happy trying to make her happy." "I make Jim happy, and he laughs," said another boy, speaking of his invalid brother; "and that makes me happy, and I laugh."

There was once a king who loved his little boy very much, and took a great deal of pains to please him. So he gave him a pony to ride, beautiful rooms to live in, pictures, books, toys without number, teachers, companions, and everything that money could buy or ingenuity devise; but for all this, the young prince was unhappy. He wore a frown wherever he went, and was always wishing for something he did not have. At length a magician came to the court. He saw the scowl on the boy's face, and said to the king: "I can make your son happy, and turn his frowns into smiles, but you must pay me a great price for telling him this secret." "All right," said the king; "whatever you ask I will give." The magician took the boy into a private room. He wrote something with a white substance on a piece of paper. He gave the boy a candle, and told him to light it and hold it under the paper, and then see what he could read. Then the magician went away. The boy did as he had been told, and the white letters turned into a beautiful blue. They formed these words: "Do a kindness to some one every day." The prince followed the advice, and became the happiest boy in the realm.

"Happiness," says one writer, "is a mosaic, composed of many smaller stones." It is the little acts of kindness, the little courtesies, the disposition to be accommodating, to be helpful, to be sympathetic, to be unselfish, to be careful not to wound the feelings, not to expose the sore spots, to be charitable of the weaknesses of others, to be considerate,—these are the little things which, added up at night, are found to be the secret of a happy day. How much greater are all these than one great act of noteworthy goodness once a year! Our lives are made up of trifles; emergencies rarely occur. "Little things, unimportant events, experiences so small as to scarcely leave a trace behind, make up the sum-total of life." And the one great thing in life is to do a little good to every one we meet. Ready sympathy, a quick eye, and a little tact, are all that are needed.

This point is happily illustrated by this report of an incident upon a train from Providence to Boston. A lady was caring for her father, whose mental faculties were weakened by age. He imagined that some imperative duty called on him to leave the swift-moving train, and his daughter could not quiet him. Just then she noticed a large man watching them over the top of his paper. As soon as he caught her eye, he rose and crossed quickly to her.

"I beg your pardon, you are in trouble. May I help you?"

She explained the situation to him.

"What is your father's name?" he asked.

She told him; and then with an encouraging smile, she spoke to her venerable father who was sitting immediately in front of her. The next moment the large man turned over the seat, and leaning toward the troubled old man, he addressed him by name, shook hands with him cordially, and engaged him in a conversation so interesting and so cleverly arranged to keep his mind occupied that the old gentleman forgot his need to leave the train, and did not think of it again until they were in Boston. There the stranger put the lady and her charge into a carriage, received her assurance that she felt perfectly safe, and was about to close the carriage door, when she remembered that she had felt so safe in the keeping of this noble-looking man that she had not even asked his name. Hastily putting her hand against the door, she said: "Pardon me, but you have rendered me such service, may I not know whom I am thanking?" The big man smiled as he turned away, and answered:—

"PHILLIPS BROOKS."

"What a gift it is," said Beecher, who was the great preacher of cheerfulness, "to make all men better and happier without knowing it! We do not suppose that flowers know how sweet they are. These roses and carnations have made me happy for a day. Yet they stand huddled together in my pitcher, without seeming to know my thoughts of them, or the gracious work they are doing. And how much more is it, to have a disposition that carries with it involuntarily sweetness, calmness, courage, hope, and happiness. Yet this is the portion of good nature in a large-minded, strong-natured man. When it has made him happy, it has scarcely begun its office. God sends a natural heart-singer—a man whose nature is large and luminous, and who, by his very carriage and spontaneous actions, calms, cheers, and helps his fellows. God bless him, for he blesses everybody!" This is just what Mr. Beecher would have said about Phillips Brooks.

And what better can be said than to compare the heart's good cheer to a floral offering? *Are not flowers appropriate gifts to persons of all ages, in any conceivable circumstances in which they are placed? So the heart's good cheer and deeds of kindness are always acceptable to children and youth, to busy men and women, to the aged, and to a world of invalids.*

"Thus live and die, O man immortal," says Dr. Chalmers. "Live for something. Do good, and leave behind you a monument of virtue, which the storms of time can never destroy. Write your name in kindness, love, and mercy, on the hearts of those who come in contact with you, and you will never be forgotten. Good deeds will shine as brightly on earth as the stars of heaven."

What is needed to round out human happiness is a well-balanced life. Not ease, not pleasure, not happiness, but a man, Nature is after. "There is," says Robert Waters, "no success without honor; no happiness without a clear conscience; no use in living at all if only for one's self. It is not at all necessary for you to make a fortune, but it is necessary, absolutely necessary, that you should become a fair-dealing, honorable, useful man, radiating goodness and cheerfulness wherever you go, and making your life a blessing."

"When a man does not find repose in himself," says a French proverb, "it is vain for him to seek it elsewhere." Happy is he who has no sense of discord with the harmony of the universe, who is open to the voices of nature and of the spiritual realm, and who sees the light that never was on sea or land. Such a life can but give expression to its inward harmony. Every pure and healthy thought, every noble aspiration for the good and the true, every longing of the heart for a higher and better life, every lofty purpose and unselfish endeavor, makes the human spirit stronger, more harmonious, and more beautiful. It is this alone that gives a self-centered confidence in one's heaven-aided powers, and a high-minded cheerfulness, like that of a celestial spirit. It is this which an old writer has called the paradise of a good conscience.

"I count this thing to be grandly true,
That a noble deed is a step toward God;
Lifting the soul from the common clod
To a purer air and a broader view.

"We rise by the things that are under our feet;
By what we have mastered of good or gain;
By the pride deposed and the passion slain,
And the vanquished ills that we hourly meet."

"My body must walk the earth," said an ancient poet, "but I can put wings on my soul, and plumes to my hardest thought." The splendors and symphonies and the ecstacies of a higher world are with us now in the rudimentary organs of eye and ear and heart. Much we have to do, much we have to love, much we have to hope for; and our "joy is the grace we say to God." "When I think upon God," said Haydn to Carpani, "my heart is so full of joy that the notes leap from my pen."

Says Gibbons:—

"Our lives are songs:
God writes the words,
And we set them to music at leisure;
And the song is sad, or the song is glad,
As we choose to fashion the measure.

"We must write the song
Whatever the words,
Whatever its rhyme or meter;
And if it is sad, we must make it glad,
And if sweet, we must make it sweeter."

VI - "Looking Pleasant"—Something to Be Worked from the Inside

*

Acting on a sudden impulse, an elderly woman, the widow of a soldier who had been killed in the Civil War, went into a photographer's to have her picture taken. She was seated before the camera wearing the same stern, hard, forbidding look that had made her an object of fear to the children living in the neighborhood, when the photographer, thrusting his head out from the black cloth, said suddenly, "Brighten the eyes a little."

She tried, but the dull and heavy look still lingered.

"Look a little pleasanter," said the photographer, in an unimpassioned but confident and commanding voice.

"See here," the woman retorted sharply, "if you think that an old woman who is dull can look bright, that one who feels cross can become pleasant every time she is told to, you don't know anything about human nature. It takes something from the outside to brighten the eye and illuminate the face."

"Oh, no, it doesn't! *It's something to be worked from the inside.* Try it again," said the photographer good-naturedly.

Something in his manner inspired faith, and she tried again, this time with better success.

"That's good! That's fine! You look twenty years younger," exclaimed the artist, as he caught the transient glow that illuminated the faded face.

She went home with a queer feeling in her heart. It was the first compliment she had received since her husband had passed away, and it left a pleasant memory behind. When she reached her little cottage, she looked long in the glass and said, "There may be something in it. But I'll wait and see the picture."

When the picture came, it was like a resurrection. The face seemed alive with the lost fires of youth. She gazed long and earnestly, then said in a clear, firm voice, "If I could do it once, I can do it again."

Approaching the little mirror above her bureau, she said, "Brighten up, Catherine," and the old light flashed up once more.

"Look a little pleasanter!" she commanded; and a calm and radiant smile diffused itself over the face.

Her neighbors, as the writer of this story has said, soon remarked the change that had come over her face: "Why, Mrs. A., you are getting young. How do you manage it?"

"*It is almost all done from the inside. You just brighten up inside and feel pleasant.*"

"Fate served me meanly, but I looked at her and laughed,
That none might know how bitter was the cup I quaffed.
Along came Joy and paused beside me where I sat,
Saying, 'I came to see what you were laughing at.'"

Every emotion tends to sculpture the body into beauty or into ugliness. Worrying, fretting, unbridled passions, petulance, discontent, every dishonest act, every falsehood, every feeling of envy, jealousy, fear,—each has its effect on the system, and acts deleteriously like a poison or a deformer of the body. Professor James of Harvard, an expert in the mental sciences, says, "Every small stroke of virtue or vice leaves its ever so little scar. Nothing we ever do is, in strict literalness, wiped out." *The way to be beautiful without is to be beautiful within.*

WORTH FIVE HUNDRED DOLLARS.

It is related that Dwight L. Moody once offered to his Northfield pupils a prize of five hundred dollars for the best thought. This took the prize: "Men grumble because God put thorns with roses; wouldn't it be better to thank God that he put roses with thorns?"

We win half the battle when we make up our minds to take the world as we find it, including the thorns. "It is," says Fontenelle, "a great obstacle to happiness to expect too much." This is what happens in real life. Watch Edison. He makes the most expensive experiments throughout a long period of time, and he expects to make them, and he never worries because he does not succeed the first time.

"I cannot but think," says Sir John Lubbock, "that the world would be better and brighter if our teachers would dwell on the duty of happiness as well as on the happiness of duty."

Oliver Wendell Holmes, in advanced years, acknowledged his debt of gratitude to the nurse of his childhood, who studiously taught him to ignore unpleasant incidents. If he stubbed his toe, or skinned his knee, or bumped his nose, his nurse would never permit his mind to dwell upon the temporary pain, but claimed his attention for some pretty object, or charming story, or happy reminiscence. To her, he said, he was largely indebted for the sunshine of a long life. It is a lesson which is easily mastered in childhood, but seldom to be learned in middle life, and never in old age.

"When I was a boy," says another author, "I was consoled for cutting my finger by having my attention called to the fact that I had not broken my arm; and when I got a cinder in my eye, I was expected to feel more comfortable because my cousin had lost his eye by an accident."

"We should brave trouble," says Beecher, "as the New England boy braves winter. The school is a mile away over the hill, yet he lingers not by the fire; but, with his books slung over his shoulder, he sets out to face the storm. When he reaches the topmost ridge, where the snow lies in drifts, and the north wind comes keen and biting, does he shrink and cower down by the fences, or run into the nearest house to warm himself? No; he buttons up his coat, and rejoices to defy the blast, and tosses the snow-wreaths with his foot; and so, erect and fearless, with strong heart and ruddy cheek, he goes on to his place at school."

Children should be taught the habit of finding pleasure everywhere; and to see the bright side of everything. "Serenity of mind comes easy to some, and hard to others. It can be taught and learned. We ought to have teachers who are able to educate us in this department of our natures quite as much as in music or art. Think of a school or classes for training men and women to carry themselves serenely amid all the trials that beset them!"

"Joy is the mainspring in the whole
Of endless Nature's calm rotation.
Joy moves the dazzling wheels that roll
In the great timepiece of Creation."
SCHILLER.

THE "DON'T WORRY" SOCIETY

was organized not long ago in New York; it is, however, just as well suited to other latitudes and longitudes. It is intended for people who "cannot help worrying."

If really you can't help it, you are in an abnormal condition, you have lost self-control,—it is a mild type of mental derangement. You must attack your bad habit of worrying as you would a disease. It is definitely something to be overcome, an infirmity that you are to get rid of.

"Be good and you will be happy," is a very old piece of advice. Mrs. Mary A. Livermore now proposes to reverse it,—"Be happy and you will be good." If unhappiness is a bad habit, you are to turn about by sheer force of will and practice cheerfulness. "Happiness is a thing to be practiced like a violin."

Not work, but worry, fretfulness, friction,—these are our foes in America. You should not go here and there, making prominent either your bad manners or a gloomy face. Who has a right to rob other people of their happiness? "Do not," says Emerson, "hang a dismal picture on your wall; and do not deal with sables and glooms in your conversation."

If you are not at the moment cheerful,—look, speak, act, as if you were. "You know I had no money, I had nothing to give but myself," said a woman who had great sorrows to bear, but who bore them cheerfully. "I formed a resolution never to sadden any one else with my troubles. I have laughed and told jokes when I could have wept. I have always smiled in the face of every misfortune. I have tried never to let any one go from my presence without a happy word or a bright thought to carry away. And happiness makes happiness. I myself am happier than I should have been had I sat down and bemoaned my fate."

"'T is easy enough to be pleasant,
When life flows along like a song;
But the man worth while is the one who will smile
When everything goes dead wrong;
For the test of the heart is trouble,
And it always comes with the years;
And the smile that is worth the praise of the earth
Is the smile that comes through tears."

A PLEASURE BOOK.

"She is an aged woman, but her face is serene and peaceful, though trouble has not passed her by. She seems utterly above the little worries and vexations which torment the average woman and leave lines of care. The Fretful Woman asked her one day the secret of her happiness; and the beautiful old face shone with joy.

"'My dear,' she said, 'I keep a Pleasure Book.'

"'A what?'

"'A Pleasure Book. Long ago I learned that there is no day so dark and gloomy that it does not contain some ray of light, and I have made it one business of my life to write down the little things which mean so much to a woman. I have a book marked for every day of every year since I left school. It is but a little thing: the new gown, the chat with a friend, the thoughtfulness of my husband, a flower, a book, a walk in the field, a letter, a concert, or a drive; but it all goes into my Pleasure Book, and, when I am inclined to fret, I read a few pages to see what a happy, blessed woman I am. You may see my treasures if you will.'

"Slowly the peevish, discontented woman turned over the book her friend brought her, reading a little here and there. One day's entries ran thus: 'Had a pleasant letter from mother. Saw a beautiful lily in a window. Found the pin I thought I had lost. Saw such a bright, happy girl on the street. Husband brought some roses in the evening.'

"Bits of verse and lines from her daily reading have gone into the Pleasure Book of this world-wise woman, until its pages are a storehouse of truth and beauty.[1]

"'Have you found a pleasure for every day?' the Fretful Woman asked.

"'For every day,' the low voice answered; 'I had to make my theory come true, you know.'"

The Fretful Woman ought to have stopped there, but did not; and she found that page where it was written—"He died with his hand in mine, and my name upon his lips." Below were the lines from Lowell:—

"Lone watcher on the mountain height:
It is right precious to behold
The first long surf of climbing light
Flood all the thirsty eat with gold;

"Yet God deems not thine aeried sight
More worthy than our twilight dim,
For meek obedience, too, is light,
And following that is finding Him."

In one of the battles of the Crimea, a cannon-ball struck inside the fort, crashing through a beautiful garden; but from the ugly chasm there burst forth a spring of water which is still flowing. And how beautiful it is, if our strange earthly sorrows become a blessing to others, through our determination to live and to do for those who need our help. Life is not given for mourning, but for unselfish service.

"Cheerfulness," says Ruskin, "is as natural to the heart of a man in strong health as color to his cheek; and wherever there is habitual gloom there must be either bad air, unwholesome food, improperly severe labor, or erring habits of life." It is an erring habit of life if we are not first of all cheerful. We are thrown into a morbid habit through circumstances utterly beyond our control, yet this fact does not change our duty toward God and toward man,—our duty to be cheerful. We are human; but it is our high privilege to lead a divine life, to accept the joy which our Lord bequeathed to his disciples.

Our trouble is that we do not half will. After a man's habits are well set, about all he can do is to sit by and observe which way he is going. Regret it as he may, how helpless is a weak man, bound by the mighty cable of habit; twisted from tiny threads which he thought were absolutely within his control. Yet a habit of happy thought would transform his life into harmony and beauty. Is not the will almost omnipotent to determine habits before they become all-powerful? What contributes more to health or happiness than a vigorous will? A habit of directing a firm and steady will upon those things which tend to produce harmony of thought will bring happiness and contentment; the will, rightly drilled,—and divinely guided,—can drive out all discordant thoughts, and usher in the reign of perpetual harmony. It is impossible to overestimate the importance of forming a habit of cheerfulness early in life. The serene optimist is one whose mind has dwelt so long upon the sunny side of life that he has acquired a habit of cheerfulness.

"Talk happiness. The world is sad enough
Without your woes. No path is wholly rough;
Look for the places that are smooth and clear,
And speak of those who rest the weary ear
Of earth, so hurt by one continuous strain
Of human discontent and grief and pain.

"Talk faith. The world is better off without
Your uttered ignorance and morbid doubt.
If you have faith in God, or man, or self,
Say so; if not, push back upon the shelf

Of silence all your thoughts till faith shall come;
No one will grieve because your lips are dumb.

"Talk health. The dreary, never-changing tale
Of mortal maladies is worn and stale.
You cannot charm, or interest, or please,
By harping on that minor chord, disease.
Say you are well, or all is well with you.
And God shall hear your words and make them true."[2]

VII - The Sunshine-Man

*

"There's the dearest little old gentleman," says James Buckham, "who goes into town every morning on the 8.30 train. I don't know his name, and yet I know him better than anybody else in town. He just radiates cheerfulness as far as you can see him. There is always a smile on his face, and I never heard him open his mouth except to say something kind, courteous, or good natured. Everybody bows to him, even strangers, and he bows to everybody, yet never with the slightest hint of presumption or familiarity. If the weather is fine, his jolly compliments make it seem finer; and if it is raining, the merry way in which he speaks of it is as good as a rainbow. Everybody who goes in on the 8.30 train knows the sunshine-man; it's his train. You just hurry up a little, and I'll show you the sunshine-man this morning. It's foggy and cold, but if one look at him doesn't cheer you up so that you'll want to whistle, then I'm no judge of human nature."

"Good morning, sir!" said Mr. Jolliboy in going to the same train.

"Why, sir, I don't know you," replied Mr. Neversmile.

"I didn't say you did, sir. Good morning, sir!"

"The inborn geniality of some people," says Whipple, "amounts to genius." "How in our troubled lives," asks J. Freeman Clarke, "could we do without these fair, sunny natures, into which on their creation-day God allowed nothing sour, acrid, or bitter to enter, but made them a perpetual solace and comfort by their cheerfulness?" There are those whose very presence carries sunshine with them wherever they go; a sunshine which means pity for the poor, sympathy for the suffering, help for the unfortunate, and benignity toward all. Everybody loves the sunny soul. His very face is a passport anywhere. All doors fly open to him. He disarms prejudice and envy, for he bears good will to everybody. He is as welcome in every household as the sunshine.

"He was quiet, cheerful, genial," says Carlyle in his "Reminiscences" concerning Edward Irving's sunny helpfulness. "His soul unruffled, clear as a mirror, honestly loving and loved, Irving's voice was to me one of blessedness and new hope."

And to William Wilberforce the poet Southey paid this tribute: "I never saw any other man who seemed to enjoy such perpetual serenity and sunshine of spirit."

"I resolved," said Tom Hood, "that, like the sun, so long as my day lasted, I would look on the bright side of everything."

When Goldsmith was in Flanders he discovered the happiest man he had ever seen. At his toil, from morning till night, he was full of song and laughter. Yet this sunny-hearted being was a slave, maimed, deformed, and wearing a chain. How well he illustrated that saying which bids us, if there is no bright side, to polish up the dark one! "Mirth is like the flash of lightning that breaks through the gloom of the clouds and glitters for a moment; cheerfulness keeps up a daylight in the soul, filling it with a steady and perpetual serenity." It is cheerfulness that has the staying quality, like the sunshine changing a world of gloom into a paradise of beauty.

The first prize at a flower-show was taken by a pale, sickly little girl, who lived in a close, dark court in the east of London. The judges asked how she could grow it in such a dingy and sunless place. She replied that a little ray of sunlight came into the court; as soon as it appeared in the morning, she put her flower beneath it, and, as it moved, moved the flower, so that she kept it in the sunlight all day.

"Water, air, and sunshine, the three greatest hygienic agents, are free, and within the reach of all." "Twelve years ago," says Walt Whitman, "I came to Camden to die. But every day I went into the country, and bathed in the sunshine, lived with the birds and squirrels, and played in the water with the fishes. I received my health from Nature."

"It is the unqualified result of all my experience with the sick," said Florence Nightingale, "that second only to their need of fresh air, is their need of light; that, after a close room, what most hurts them is a dark room; and that it is not only light, but direct sunshine they want."

"Sunlight," says Dr. L. W. Curtis, in "Health Culture," "has much to do in keeping air in a healthy condition. No plant can grow in the dark, neither can man remain healthy in a dark, ill-ventilated room. When the first asylum for the blind was erected in Massachusetts, the committee decided to save expense by not having any windows. They reasoned that, as the patients could not see, there was no need of any light. It was built without windows, but ventilation was well provided for, and the poor sightless patients were domiciled in the house. But things did not go well: one after another began to sicken, and great languor fell upon them; they felt distressed and restless, craving something, they hardly knew what. After two had died and all were ill, the committee decided to have windows. The sunlight poured in, and the white faces recovered their color; their flagging energies and depressed spirits revived, and health was restored."

The sun, making all living things to grow, exerts its happiest influence in cheering the mind of man and making his heart glad, and if a man has sunshine in his soul he will go on his way rejoicing; content to look forward if under a cloud, not bating one jot of heart or hope if for a moment cast down; honoring his occupation, whatever it be; rendering even rags respectable by the way he wears them; and not only happy himself, but giving happiness to others.

How a man's face shines when illuminated by a great moral motive! and his manner, too, is touched with the grace of light.

"Nothing will supply the want of sunshine to peaches," said Emerson, "and to make knowledge valuable you must have the cheerfulness of wisdom."

"Wondrous is the strength of cheerfulness," said Carlyle; "altogether past calculation its powers of endurance. Efforts to be permanently useful must be uniformly joyous,—a spirit all sunshine, graceful from very gladness, beautiful because bright."

"The cheerful man carries with him perpetually, in his presence and personality, an influence that acts upon others as summer warmth on the fields and forests. It wakes up and calls out the best that is in them. It makes them stronger, braver, and happier. Such a man makes a little spot of this world a lighter, brighter, warmer place for other people to live in. To meet him in the morning is to get inspiration which makes all the day's struggles and tasks easier. His hearty handshake puts a thrill of new vigor into your veins. After talking with him for a few minutes, you feel an exhilaration of spirits, a quickening of energy, a renewal of zest and interest in living, and are ready for any duty or service."

"Great hearts there are among men," says Hillis, of Plymouth pulpit; "they carry a volume of manhood; their presence is sunshine; their coming changes our climate; they oil the bearings of life; their shadow always falls behind them; they make right living easy. Blessed are the happiness-makers: they represent the best forces in civilization!"

If refined manners reprove us a little for ill-timed laughter, a smiling face kindled by a smiling heart is always in order. Who can ever forget Emerson's smile? It was a perpetual benediction upon all who knew him. A smile is said to be to the human countenance what sunshine is to the landscape. Or a smile is called the rainbow of the face.

"This is a dark world to many people," says a suggestive modern writer, "a world of chills, a world of fogs, a world of wet blankets. Nine-tenths of the men we meet need encouragement. Your work is so urgent that you have no time to stop and speak to the people, but every day you meet scores, perhaps hundreds and thousands of persons, upon whom you might have direct and immediate influence. 'How? How?' you cry out. We answer: By the grace of physiognomy. There is nothing more catching than a face with a lantern behind it, shining clear through. We have no admiration for a face with a dry smile, meaning no more than the grin of a false face. But a smile written by the hand of God, as an index finger or table of contents, to whole volumes of good feeling within, is a benediction. You say: 'My face is hard and lacking in mobility, and my benignant feelings are not observable in the facial proportions.' We do not believe you. Freshness and geniality of the soul are so subtle and pervading that they will, at some eye or mouth corner, leak out. Set behind your face a feeling of gratitude to God and kindliness toward man, and you will every day preach a sermon long as the streets you walk, a sermon with as many heads as the number of people you meet, and differing from other sermons in the fact that the longer it is the better. The reason that there are so many sour faces, so many frowning faces, so many dull faces, is because men consent to be acrid and petulant, and stupid. The way to improve your face is to improve your disposition. Attractiveness of physiognomy does not depend on regularity of features. We know persons whose brows are shaggy, eyes oblique, noses ominously longitudinal, and mouths straggling along in unusual and unexpected directions; and yet they are men and women of so much soul that we love to look upon them, and their faces are sweet evangels."

It was N. P. Willis, I think, who added to the beatitudes—"Blessed are the joy-makers." "And this is why all the world loves little children, who are always ready to have 'a sunshine party,'—little children bubbling over with fun, as a bobolink with song.

"How well we remember it all!—the long gone years of our own childhood, and the households of joyous children we have known in later years. Joy-makers are the children still,—some of them in unending scenes of light. I saw but yesterday this epitaph at Mount Auburn,—'She was so pleasant': sunny-hearted in life, and now alive forever more in light supernal.

"How can we then but rejoice with joy unspeakable, as the children of immortality; living habitually above the gloom and damps of earth, and leading lives of ministration; bestowing everywhere sweetness and light,— radiating upon the earth something of the beauty of the unseen world."

What is a sunny temper but "a talisman more powerful than wealth, more precious than rubies"? What is it but "an aroma whose fragrance fills the air with the odors of Paradise"?

"I am so full of happiness," said a little child, "that I could not be any happier unless I could grow." And she bade "Good morning" to her sweet singing bird, and "Good morning" to the sun; then she asked her mother's permission, and softly, reverently, gladly bade "Good morning to God,"— and why should she not?

Was it not Goethe who represented a journey that followed the sunshine round the world, forever bathed in light? And Longfellow sang:

"'T is always morning somewhere; and above
The awakening continents, from shore to shore,
Somewhere the birds are singing evermore."

"The darkness past, we mount the radiant skies,
And changeless day is ours; we hear the songs
Of higher spheres, the light divine our eyes
Behold and sunlight robes of countless throngs
Who dwell in light; we seek, with joyous quest,
God's service sweet to wipe all tears away,
And list we every hour, with eager zest,
For high command to toils that God has blest:
So fill we full our endless sunshine day."

*** * * *

www.ingramcontent.com/pod-product-compliance
Lightning Source LLC
Chambersburg PA
CBHW081732100526
44591CB00016B/2591